CRAFTS FOR ALL SEASONS

CREATING BY
RECYCLING

Published by Blackbirch Press, Inc.
260 Amity Road
Woodbridge, CT 06525

©2000 by Blackbirch Press, Inc.
First Edition

Originally published as: *Crea y recicla* by Anna Llimós and Laia Sadurní; photography by Nos y Soto; illustration by Núria Giralt

Original Copyright: ©1999 Parramón Ediciones, S.A., World Rights, Published by Parramón Ediciones, S.A., Barcelona, Spain.

e-mail: staff@blackbirch.com
Web site: www.blackbirch.com

Printed in Spain

10 9 8 7 6 5 4 3 2 1

Library of Congress Cataloging-in-Publication Data
Llimós, Anna.
[Crea y recicla. English]
Creating by recycling / by Anna Llimós and Laia Sadurní.
   p.   cm. — (Crafts for all seasons)
Includes bibliographical references and index.
Summary: Provides instructions for a variety of craft projects using such recycled items as foam trays, empty soda cans, cardboard tubes, plastic bottles and pieces of cloth.
ISBN 1-56711-436-9
1. Handicraft—Juvenile literature. 2. Recycling (Waste, etc.)—Juvenile literature. 3. Plastic bottle craft—Juvenile literature. [1. Handicraft. 2. Recycling (Waste, etc.)] I. Sadurní, Laia. II. Title III. Series: Crafts for all seasons (Woodbridge, Conn.)
TT160.L5913   2000   98-38943
745.5—dc21   CIP
                                                      AC

Contents

CRAFTS FOR ALL SEASONS

CREATING BY
RECYCLING

BLACKBIRCH PRESS, INC.
WOODBRIDGE, CONNECTICUT

A Marvelous Motor-Car ✂

☞ YOU'LL NEED:
two clean and dry juice or milk boxes; some thin, flexible wire; four matching bottle caps; modeling clay; scissors; a magic marker; adhesive tape; and paint.

1. Draw the front and the windows of your car on one of the empty boxes.

2. Cut along the lines you've drawn. Ask an adult for help, if you need to.

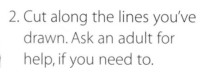

3. To complete the front of the car, cut out the side of the second box. Then fold it and attach it to the front opening with adhesive tape.

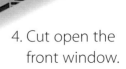

4. Cut open the front window.

5. Paint the car with your favorite color. Make two small holes near the bottom of each side for the wires that will hold the wheels together.

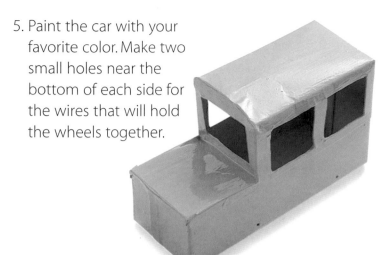

6. Make a hole in the center of each of the four caps. (Ask an adult for help, if you need to.)

7. Run a piece of wire through a cap, then through two facing holes on the car's sides. Place another cap on the other end of the wire. Do the same for the other two wheels. Cover the wire ends with little balls of modeling clay.

8. Step on the gas! Full speed ahead!

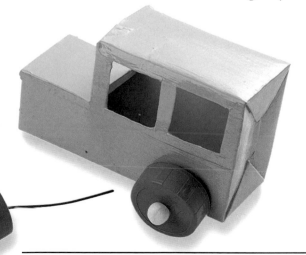

💡 *Use your imagination:* *You can use juice boxes or milk containers to make all sorts of vehicles. Try making a train with small bottle caps, a bus with medium size caps, or use really big bottle caps to make a tractor!*

An Egg-Cellent Eggodile ✂

☛ YOU'LL NEED: the top of a container for a dozen eggs, both parts of a container for half a dozen eggs, four empty toilet paper rolls, green, black, and white paint, red or pink construction paper, a needle with thread or string, glue, adhesive tape, and varnish (optional).

1. Paint all the egg containers and rolls green. When the green has dried, paint white nails on the four rolls, which will be the legs. When the paint dries, you can varnish the rolls, if you like.

2. With thread or string, tie together the two parts of the smaller container to form the head. You may want to ask an adult for help.

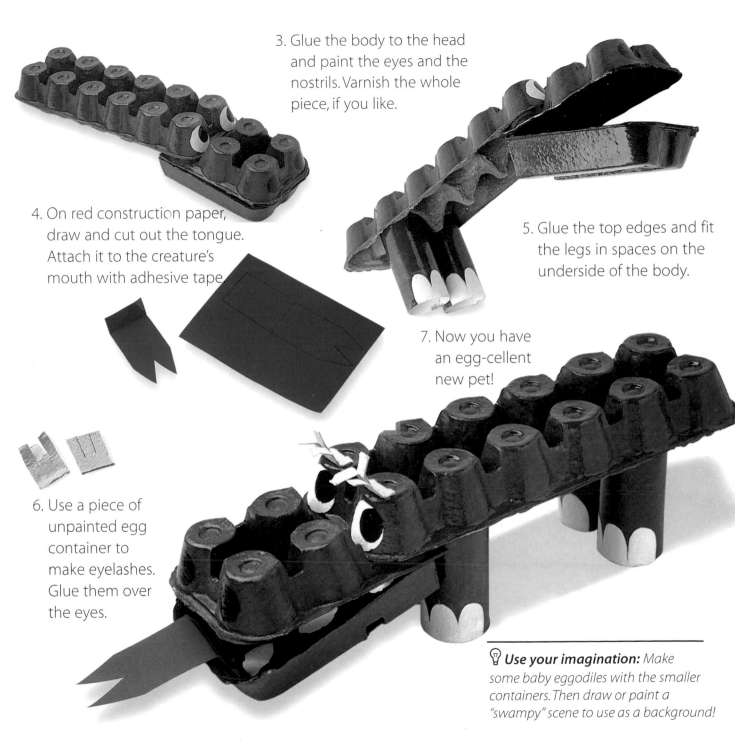

3. Glue the body to the head and paint the eyes and the nostrils. Varnish the whole piece, if you like.

4. On red construction paper, draw and cut out the tongue. Attach it to the creature's mouth with adhesive tape.

5. Glue the top edges and fit the legs in spaces on the underside of the body.

7. Now you have an egg-cellent new pet!

6. Use a piece of unpainted egg container to make eyelashes. Glue them over the eyes.

💡 *Use your imagination:* Make some baby eggodiles with the smaller containers. Then draw or paint a "swampy" scene to use as a background!

A Perfect Personal Organizer ✂

☞ **YOU'LL NEED:** *various-sized empty matchboxes, bobby pins, buttons, colored adhesive tape or colored construction paper, various paints, and glue. Note: An adult will need wire cutters or pruning shears.*

1. Paint the inner parts of the matchboxes different colors. Let the paint dry completely.

2. Use colored adhesive tape or glue construction paper to line the matchbox sides. Then paint the entire exterior of the boxes.

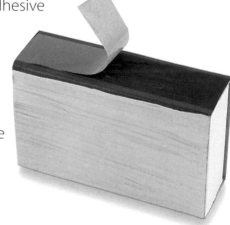

3. Find buttons of different colors and sizes. Have an adult use wire cutters to cut off the closed end of several bobby pins. Insert the bobby pins into the buttonholes. You can also use twist-ties, if your prefer.

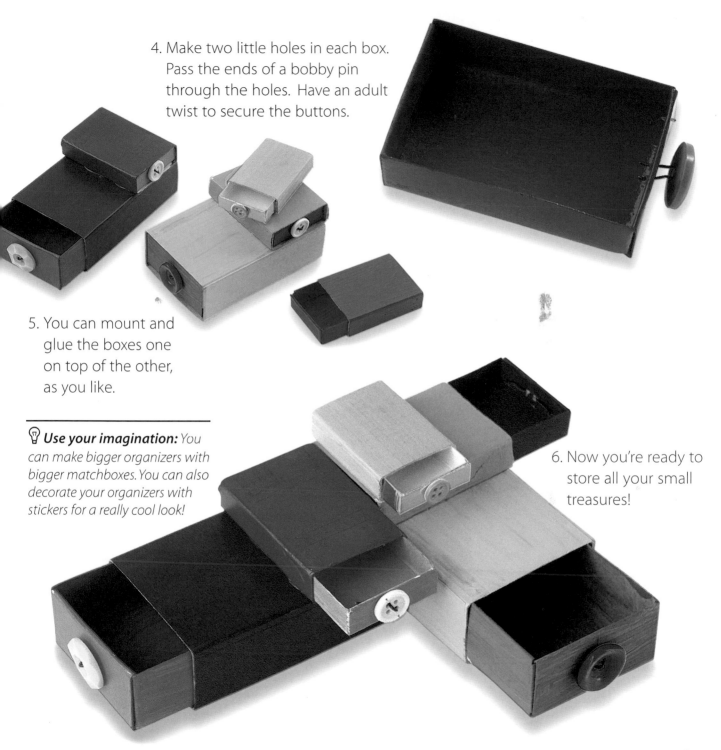

4. Make two little holes in each box. Pass the ends of a bobby pin through the holes. Have an adult twist to secure the buttons.

5. You can mount and glue the boxes one on top of the other, as you like.

💡 **Use your imagination:** *You can make bigger organizers with bigger matchboxes. You can also decorate your organizers with stickers for a really cool look!*

6. Now you're ready to store all your small treasures!

9

Inter-Galactic Communications Center

1. Paint all the items silver.

2. Cut a piece of blue cellophane. Apply glue to the upper rim of the pudding container and press the cellophane over it.

☛ YOU'LL NEED: a cardboard or foam tray, a toilet paper roll, two yogurt containers, a square pudding or fruit container, colored cellophane and tissue paper, toothpicks, modeling clay, buttons, an empty box, aluminum foil, silver paint, glue, and empty tablet containers (optional).

3. When the glue dries, cut off the excess cellophane.

4. For the keyboard, paint an empty box and glue buttons onto it, or ask an adult to give you an empty foil-strip tablet container and its box.

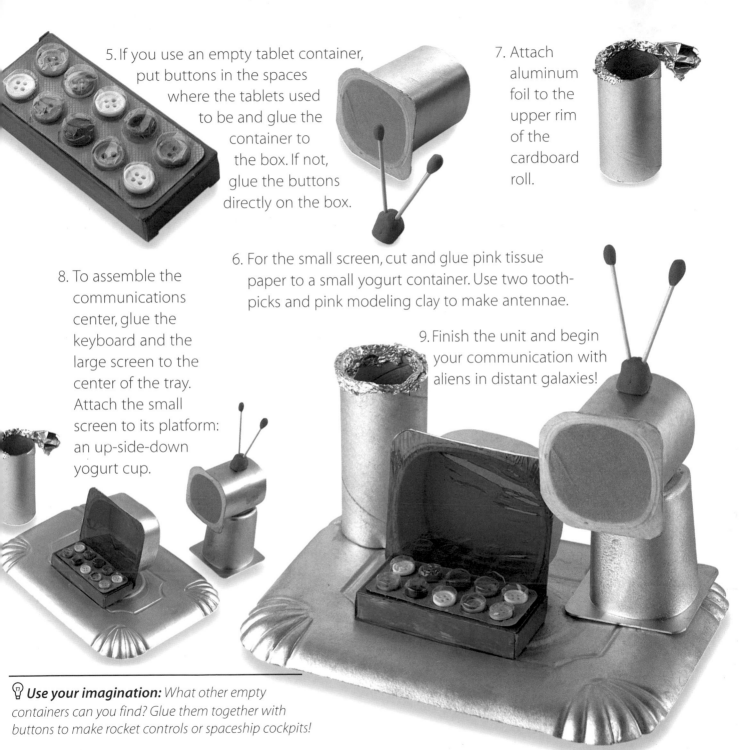

5. If you use an empty tablet container, put buttons in the spaces where the tablets used to be and glue the container to the box. If not, glue the buttons directly on the box.

7. Attach aluminum foil to the upper rim of the cardboard roll.

6. For the small screen, cut and glue pink tissue paper to a small yogurt container. Use two toothpicks and pink modeling clay to make antennae.

8. To assemble the communications center, glue the keyboard and the large screen to the center of the tray. Attach the small screen to its platform: an up-side-down yogurt cup.

9. Finish the unit and begin your communication with aliens in distant galaxies!

💡 **Use your imagination:** *What other empty containers can you find? Glue them together with buttons to make rocket controls or spaceship cockpits!*

A Scary Spider Puppet

1. Wash your soda can out well, and have an adult remove the pop-top.

☞ *YOU'LL NEED: an empty soda can, two bottle caps, colored cotton balls, two clear plastic gloves, glue, black marker, adhesive tape, an empty yogurt, pudding, or fruit container.*

2. Glue multi-colored cotton balls to the outside of the can, except for the top and a strip along the side.

3. Fill two clear plastic gloves with cotton balls.

4. Use adhesive tape to close off the end of one glove. Glue it to the uncovered strip on the side of the can.

5. Do the same with the other glove. Cover the area where the gloves meet with glued-on cotton balls. Make sure the two thumbs stick out over the face like antennae.

6. Find two bottle caps and draw eyes on the insides with a magic marker. Glue the caps over the opening of the can.

7. You can make a pedestal for your spider out of a small yogurt container, or hang it from an elastic string or large rubber band.

💡 **Use your imagination:** *You can make other glove creatures, too. Try making an octopus or different kinds of alien life forms.*

13

A Mini Merry-Go-Round

☛ **YOU'LL NEED: a plastic flower pot, five different plastic caps (from aerosol cans), stickers, paints and brushes, modeling clay, a wooden rod or dowel, wide ribbon, scissors, and glue.**

1. Have an adult make a hole the size of a finger in the center of a round cardboard plate; make three other evenly spaced holes on the edge of the plate.

2. Draw a star on the plate and paint it.

3. Decorate each bottle cap with stickers. When the paint on the plate dries, glue a bottle cap to each point of the star.

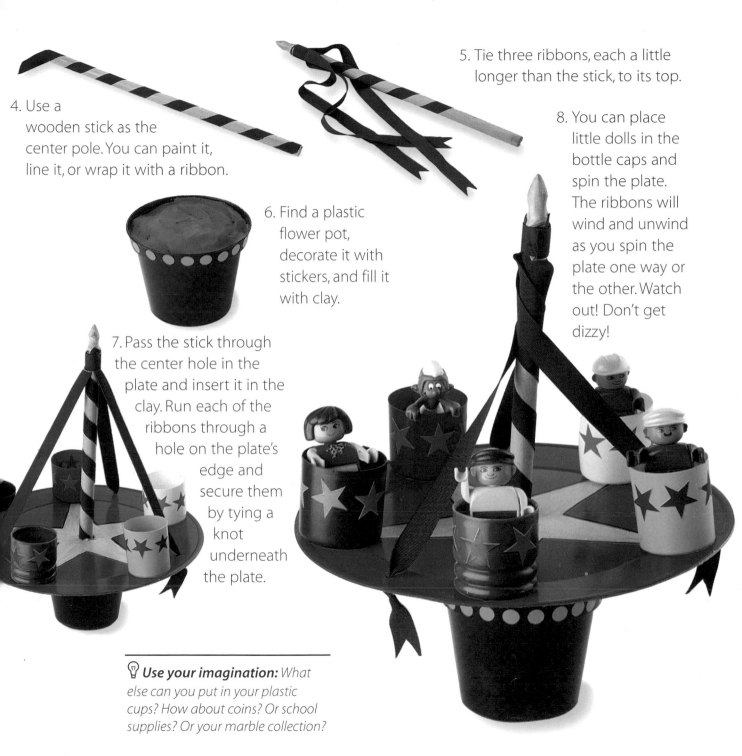

4. Use a wooden stick as the center pole. You can paint it, line it, or wrap it with a ribbon.

5. Tie three ribbons, each a little longer than the stick, to its top.

6. Find a plastic flower pot, decorate it with stickers, and fill it with clay.

7. Pass the stick through the center hole in the plate and insert it in the clay. Run each of the ribbons through a hole on the plate's edge and secure them by tying a knot underneath the plate.

8. You can place little dolls in the bottle caps and spin the plate. The ribbons will wind and unwind as you spin the plate one way or the other. Watch out! Don't get dizzy!

💡 **Use your imagination:** *What else can you put in your plastic cups? How about coins? Or school supplies? Or your marble collection?*

15

A FotoFish Fun Frame

1. Draw the fish on the tray and cut it out. The fish should be a little smaller than the photograph you want to frame.

☛ **YOU'LL NEED:** *a styrofoam tray, colored tissue paper, glue stick, and varnish.*

2. Cut different-colored tissue paper into little pieces.

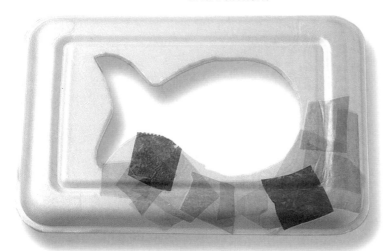

3. Using glue stick, glue both sides of the tissue paper to the tray so that they overlap a little.

4. Also cover the fish cut-out, which will serve as the frame's stand.

5. After you've covered the frame and the fish, varnish both.

6. Let the pieces dry, then glue the fish to the back and use it to hold up the frame.

7. Attach the photo to the back of the frame with adhesive tape. Pretty fishy, isn't it?

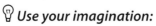

💡 *Use your imagination:*
You can cut out any kind of shape to make your frame. Try a star, a sun, a flower, or make a bunch or smaller openings for a multi-photo frame.

Totally Terrific Tubeball

☞ **YOU'LL NEED: an empty toilet paper roll, construction paper, cord, felt or craft paper, clay, scissors, and glue.**

1. Trace the end of the empty roll onto construction paper.

2. Draw triangles around the circle to make a sun. Cut it out.

3. Make a hole in the center of the cut-out. Run a piece of cord through it. Knot the end of the cord so it won't come out of the hole. Attach the cut-out to the roll by bending the triangles over and applying adhesive tape.

4. Use glue and a piece of old denim or other thick fabric to cover the roll.

5. Line the top and bottom of the roll with different color felt.

6. Tie a big knot on the end of your cord and mold some modeling clay around it in the shape of a small ball.

7. Now go for a slam-dunk!

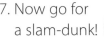

Jolly Juggling Balls

☞ **YOU'LL NEED: three small plastic bags, rice or bird seed, balloons of different colors, and scissors.**

1. Fill the plastic bags with rice or bird seed.

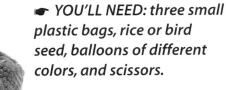

2. Take one balloon, open it wide and insert one of the bags. Cut off the neck of the balloon.

3. Pick a different color balloon, insert the ball, and cut off the neck of the balloon.

4. Use scissors to cut holes in the upper balloon. So that you don't cut the first balloon, pinch the upper one, lift it, roll it, and cut carefully.

5. Repeat steps 4 and 5, using another balloon.

6. Make three different color balls in the same way. Use them to practice juggling and start your own circus act!

Personal Piggy Bank

1. If the bottle is too long, have an adult cut it into three parts, as shown. Put the middle part into your recycling bin.

☛ **YOU'LL NEED: a clean plastic bottle with its cap, two corks, tissue paper or construction paper, wide ribbon (optional), round stickers, black marker, pink or red paint, and glue.**

2. Have an adult cut a small slot in the upper part. Join the two parts with adhesive tape.

3. Have an adult cut the two corks in half. These will be the four legs.

4. Paint the four legs and the bottle-cap snout pink or red.

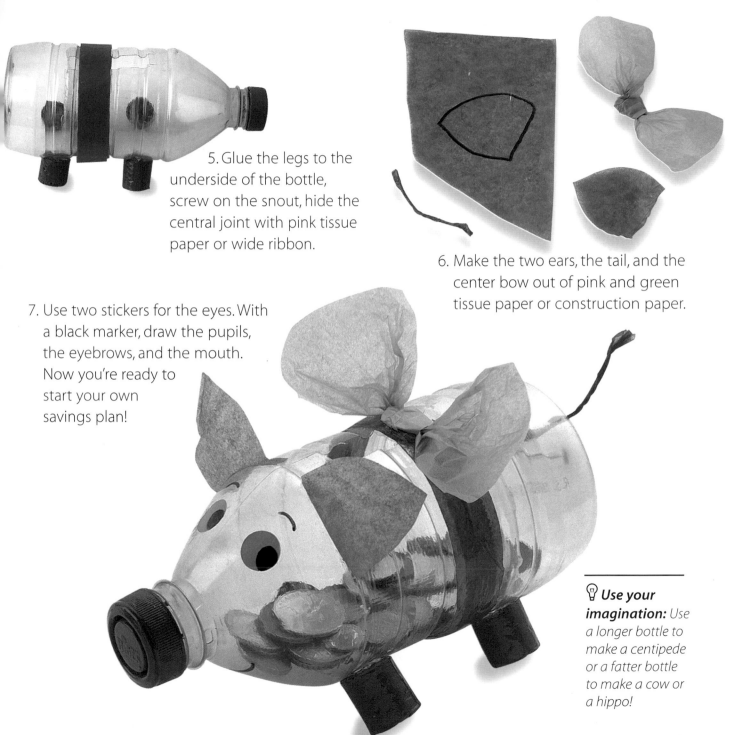

5. Glue the legs to the underside of the bottle, screw on the snout, hide the central joint with pink tissue paper or wide ribbon.

6. Make the two ears, the tail, and the center bow out of pink and green tissue paper or construction paper.

7. Use two stickers for the eyes. With a black marker, draw the pupils, the eyebrows, and the mouth. Now you're ready to start your own savings plan!

💡 *Use your imagination: Use a longer bottle to make a centipede or a fatter bottle to make a cow or a hippo!*

Portable Pocket Wall Hanger

☛ **YOU'LL NEED: A long strip cut out of an old sheet or other cloth, two pairs of old jeans or jean skirts (that you plan to throw away), watercolor paints and brushes, two sticks or reeds, cord or string, scissors, and glue.**

1. Paint the strip in various colors using diluted watercolor paints.

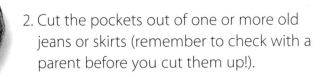

2. Cut the pockets out of one or more old jeans or skirts (remember to check with a parent before you cut them up!).

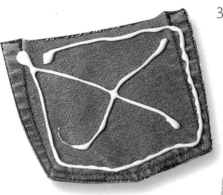

3. Glue the pockets to the cloth strip with a lot of glue.

4. Leave spaces at the top and bottom of the strip.

5. Find two reeds or sticks and glue them to each end of the strip.

6. Tie a cord to the upper stick and hang the strip in your room. Now your things will always be within easy reach!

💡 **Use your imagination:**
You can cut and glue other fabrics to use as pockets, too. Old shirts or towels work well, and so do old tablecloths or cloth napkins.

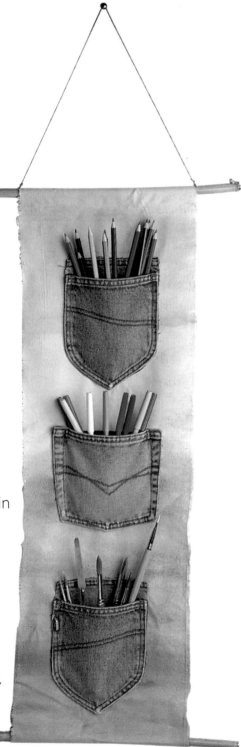

23

Letter Perfect Pencil Holder

☛ **YOU'LL NEED:**
A flat, round cheese box or two tops from boxes of oats with labels removed, cut out letters from magazine pages, several toilet paper and paper towel rolls, paints and brushes, and glue.

1. Cut the toilet paper and paper towel rolls into different sizes.

2. Glue three different size rolls to the top of the cheese box or oats lids.

3. If you're using oats lids, make a few snips in the top piece. This will help it fit over the bottom piece. Paint the inside of the box one color, and the outside of the box with the rolls, another color.

4. Decorate the holder by gluing on letters you've cut out of magazines.

5. You can also decorate with designs made out of colored thread or string.

6. Now place it on your desk, fill it up with supplies, and get down to work!

💡 **Use your imagination:** *You can decorate your holder with almost anything—cut out pictures of animals or people from magazines, cut up old photos; or use stickers or glitter glue for another cool look!*

A Jumpy Jack-in-the-Box

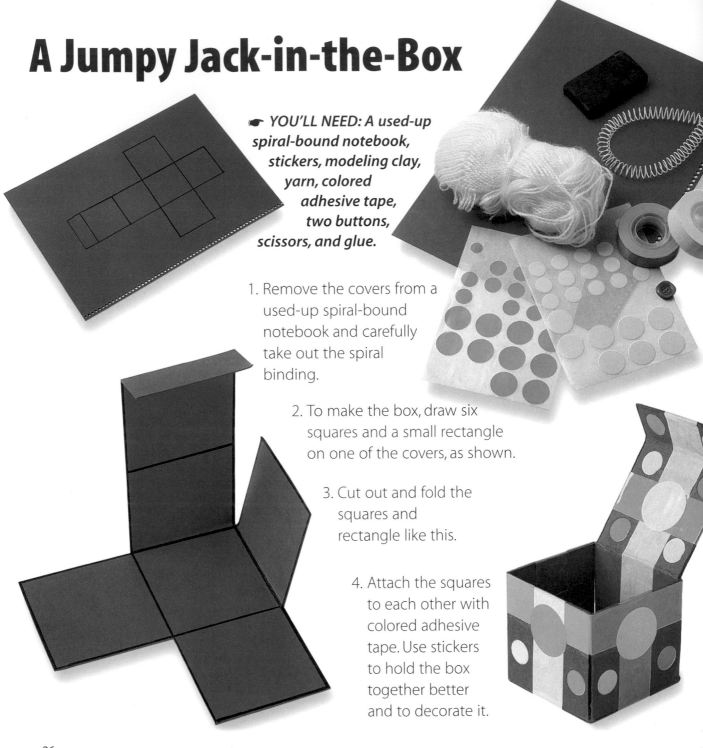

☛ **YOU'LL NEED: A used-up spiral-bound notebook, stickers, modeling clay, yarn, colored adhesive tape, two buttons, scissors, and glue.**

1. Remove the covers from a used-up spiral-bound notebook and carefully take out the spiral binding.

2. To make the box, draw six squares and a small rectangle on one of the covers, as shown.

3. Cut out and fold the squares and rectangle like this.

4. Attach the squares to each other with colored adhesive tape. Use stickers to hold the box together better and to decorate it.

5. Stick one end of the spiral into the center of a cube of modeling clay.

6. Wind yarn around a piece of construction paper. Cut it on one side and tie it on the other side with a piece of yarn so that it forms a puff.

7. Glue two buttons to the puff and glue the puff to the other end of the spiral. You can now place your little monster in the box.

8. Close the box and ask someone to open it. When they do, they're in for a surprise!

💡 *Use your imagination:* *Instead of yarn, you can use an old rolled-up sock for your monster head— or how about a small toy animal?*

A Shoebox Circus

☛ **YOU'LL NEED: A shoebox, stickers, corks, clothespin halves, thumbtacks, colored adhesive tape, string or wire cord, yarn, bobby pins or paper clips, construction paper, modeling clay, and glue.**

1. Paint the inside of your shoebox and decorate it with stickers. Line the outside with pieces of cloth and colored adhesive tape.

2. To make the tight rope, run a cord through the box. For the trapeze, tie two short lengths of cord to half a clothespin and fasten them to the upper part of the box.

3. Paint the inside of the box top green, cut two corners, and attach the resulting flap to the box with adhesive tape.

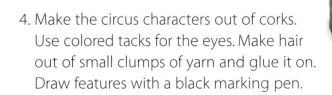

4. Make the circus characters out of corks. Use colored tacks for the eyes. Make hair out of small clumps of yarn and glue it on. Draw features with a black marking pen.

7. For the elephant, cut two ears out of construction paper and a trunk out of wire. Use half a cork, adhesive tape, and modeling clay to make a pedestal.

5. Give the tight-rope walker two arms made of bobby pins or paper clips.

6. Glue a character to the half clothes pin and it's ready to swing.

8. Paint a big sign for your magic circus on the outside of the box top. Now start selling tickets to your big show!

💡 **Use your imagination:** *You can use the same materials to make a theater with characters or a stage for a rock band!*

WHERE TO GET SUPPLIES

Art & Woodcrafters Supply, Inc.

www.artwoodcrafter.com

Order a catalog or browse online for many different craft supplies.

Craft Supplies

www.craftsfaironline.com/Supplies.html

This online craft store features many different sites, each featuring products for specific hobbies.

Darice, Inc.

21160 Drake Road

Strongsville, OH 44136-6699

www.darice.com

Order a catalog or browse online for many different craft supplies.

Making Friends

www.makingfriends.com

Offers many kits and products for children's crafts.

National Artcraft

7996 Darrow Road

Twinsburg, OH 44087

www.nationalartcraft.com

This craft store features many products available through its catalog or online.

FOR MORE INFORMATION

Books

Chapman, Gillian. *Autumn* (Seasonal Crafts). Chatham, NJ: Raintree/Steck Vaughn, 1997.

Chapman, Gillian. Pam Robson (Contributor). *Art From Fabric: With Projects Using Rags, Old Clothes, and Remnants.* New York, NY: Thomson Learning, 1995.

Connor, Nikki. Sarah Jean Neaves (Illustrator). *Cardboard Boxes* (Creating Crafts From). Providence, RI: Copper Beech Books, 1996.

Gordon, Lynn. *52 Great Art Projects For Kids.* San Francisco, CA: Chronicle Books, 1996.

King, Penny. Clare Roundhill (Contributor). *Animals* (Artists' Workshop). New York, NY: Crabtree Publishing, 1996.

Ross, Kathy. Sharon Lane Holm (Illustrator). *The Best Holiday Crafts Ever.* Brookfield, CT: Millbrook Publishing, 1996.

Smith, Alistair. *Big Book of Papercraft.* Newton, MA: Educational Development Center, 1996.

Videos

Blue's Clues Arts & Crafts. Nickelodeon. (1998).

Web Sites

Crafts For Kids
www.craftsforkids.miningco.com/mbody.htm
Many different arts and crafts activities are explained in detail.

Family Crafts
www.family.go.com
Search for crafts by age group. Projects include instructions, supply list, and helpful tips.

KinderCrafts
www.EnchantedLearning.com/Crafts
Step-by-step instructions explain how to make animal, dinosaur, box, and paper crafts, plus much more.

Making Friends
www.makingfriends.com
Contains hundreds of craft ideas with detailed instructions for children ages 2 to 12, including paper dolls, summer crafts, yucky stuff, and holiday crafts.

INDEX